Forgiveness and Love Conquers All

Healing the Emotional Self

Inspiration Mini-series

Forgiveness and Love Conquers All

Healing the Emotional Self

Stephen Richards

Inspiration Mini-series

First edition
Published in Great Britain
By Mirage Publishing 2011

First published in paperback 2011

A CIP catalogue record for this book
Is available from the British Library.

ISBN: 978-1-90257-873-6

Mirage Publishing
PO Box 161
Gateshead
NE8 4WW
Great Britain

Printed and bound in Great Britain by

Book Printing UK
Remus House, Coltsfoot Drive, Woodston, Peterborough, PE2 9JX, UK

Layout by Artistic Director Sharon Anderson

Papers used in the production of this book are recycled, thus reducing environmental depletion.

For all 'Big Issue' sellers, for they have truly forgiven.

Contents

Disclaimer

Disclaimer: the entire contents of this book are based upon research conducted by the author, unless otherwise noted. The publisher, the author, the distributors and bookstores present this information for educational purposes only. Any exercises presented here, either physical or mental, are to be practiced with caution. Should you experience any discomfort or trauma from any of the processes involved you are advised to stop. This information is not intended to diagnose or prescribe for medical or psychological conditions or to claim to prevent, treat, mitigate or cure such conditions. The author and the publisher are not making an attempt to recommend specific products as treatment of disease, and neither do they have any financial interest in the sale of the substances described in this book. In presenting this information, no attempt is being made to provide diagnosis, care, treatment or rehabilitation of individuals, or apply medical, mental health or human development principles, to provide diagnosing, treating, operating or prescribing for any human disease, pain, injury, deformity or physical condition. The information contained herein is not intended to replace a one-on-one relationship with a doctor or qualified health care professional. Therefore, the reader should be made aware that this information is not intended as medical advice, but rather a sharing of knowledge and information from the research and experience of the author. The publisher and the author encourage you to make your own health care decisions based upon your research and in partnership with a qualified health care professional. You and only you are responsible if you choose to do anything based on what you read.

INTRODUCTION

What exactly is forgiveness?

A good number of people have suffered various forms of troubles arising from neglect from an early age, persecution or unfair treatment resulting from gruesome crimes, wars, political persecution, social discrimination and more besides. Such people have, in their wake, a decision to make; whether to pardon whoever inflicted such pain on them or to simply harbour the anger they feel for such people. There are no two ways about it.

Failing to forgive will lead to a host of adverse feelings and, therefore, whoever has suffered any undesirable condition or situation inflicted upon them by another party needs to think of forgiving that other party - an essential part of getting over the hurt and pain.

A wonderful and insightful quote from an unknown source states:

To forgive is to set a prisoner free and discover the prisoner was you.

All human beings are liable to making mistakes, therefore need to learn to know that while they may make mistakes, other people too may make mistakes and for us all to co-exist, some sort of truce has to be called. This book demystifies the issue of forgiveness by offering plausible steps you will use as you weed out any resentment you feel towards the person who has wronged you.

The practice of forgiving is a chronological practice that begins with excusing someone. It may not exactly require for you to pardon something they have done against you, but it will require that you start to distance yourself from feelings of seeing red or feeling extremely irate. These feelings of dislike and anger can have a very strong hold on a person; both inside and outside.

In many cases it is these undesirable feelings that will drive us to extremes of feeling like the whole world is crushing down on us. As human beings, we are custom made to be happy. Why then would we want to change the order of things by not being happy? Being in sync with everything and everybody around us is a great contributing factor to living a happy and fulfilled life.

Before you proceed to read this book, it is worthwhile to have an open mind so that eventually you will see beyond the pain and hatred that your emotions are blocking your foresight with. This book will give you something you hitherto did not have – the ability to be able to forgive without second thoughts and the ability to realise that the pain we feel is simply because we do not forgive.

It is true that what affects us from the outside is bound to create a great instability within us; however, our responses create more of an impact when it comes to determining our happiness levels. What other people do is beyond our area of jurisdiction and we have to come to terms with the fact that not all people can be as humane, good or caring and understanding as we want them to be.

Due to the need to co-exist with these inhuman and inconsiderate people, we will obviously be disturbed by their acts; something which if we look at closely, actually means that we too could be affecting some other people negatively every once in a while. The only way one can trace their way back to real and true happiness and joy is through forgiveness.

Forgiveness and Love Conquers All

Later, in this book, you will encounter a breakdown of most of the basic impediments to forgiveness, the repercussions of failing to forgive and the fruits of forgiveness.

In order to make inroads into forgiveness, you have to locate a situation or scenario that will render you a proper journey through all the emotional phases, right from the pain through to the healing. Part of the healing process involves learning from the mistakes you make. If you do not learn, you are bound to go through similar experiences and sometimes the new experience is twice as painful as the first.

Just out of interest, there are certain situations when you should shelve the issue of forgiveness whereby someone suffering mental health problems or because of a temporary loss of sanity on their behalf or even through no fault of their own by virtue of the situation that they are in, that they have wronged against you.

Use your judgement in weighing up the situation. Obviously you can easily forgive a child who has made an academic mistake, but perhaps not forgive an adult as easily or readily for the same thing.

Before making a snap judgement, ask yourself if it really is something that has hurt you or simply just made you angry at yourself for allowing it to happen. It's amazing what 'sleeping on it' can do. A new day sees a new beginning.

Always seek to remedy the situation as soon as possible, and that way it can be forgotten and you can get on with your life. Allowing situations to drag on can drag you down like a millstone around your neck. Use forgiveness as a stepping stone to freeing yourself of the burden of worry or of carrying bitterness around with you. Carrying bitterness around will only be contagious in what you do, so nip it in the bud at an early stage.

Finally, do not allow yourself to be pulled into the role of embracing victimship as some sort of badge of honour to wear or flash around at any opportunity. The world is full of victims; don't add to the growing culture of "I've a story to tell", well not unless it's a story to help others overcome situations or as a warning.

CHAPTER 1

CLAIMING AND VALIDATING FALSE VICTIMSHIP

The truth is, forgiving is a rather difficult concept to grasp. It is often imagined that when you forgive, you have to reconcile with someone and yet this is a larger team in which forgiveness is just a player.

Forgiveness does carry with it numerous obstacles and one may well be surprised why many people find it a very difficult hurdle to jump over. Every human being will find it difficult to deal with. The trouble is that we are often so convinced that we are so hurt and in pain, so much so, that we opt not to forgive.

If we studied the issue of forgiveness with a wider perspective, we are bound to opt for it after all. Being in a bad mood is not anything a sane person would desire at any time. However, even knowing this, our sight is normally blocked by the fact that we feel extremely let down and in pain at that point in time.

The inner voice will sometimes want to exalt itself and continue insisting that it has been hurt so bad that it can *not* forgive. Often, it puts us in the spotlight as the victim – something which the ego is very much interested in. Therefore all empathy and sympathy is directed our way and we feel like we are the centre of attention.

'Not to forgive is to be imprisoned by the past, by old grievances that do not permit life to proceed with new business. Not to forgive is to yield oneself to another's

control... to be locked into a sequence of act and response, of outrage and revenge, tit for tat, escalating always. The present is endlessly overwhelmed and devoured by the past. Forgiveness frees the forgiver. It extracts the forgiver from someone else's nightmare.'

- Lance Morrow

The issue of sympathy

Many a time, it is reassuring to have people pour accolades of self righteousness on us by constantly reminding us that we are the ones in the right and they are in the wrong. This sympathy will offer some comfort, but only momentarily.

Counting on sympathy is really just treating the symptom of something and not really treating the real problem - it will only relieve you for a short time. Forgiveness on the other hand is more deep rooted and will sort out the real cause of the problem, thus eliminating all symptoms as well.

I am *THE* victim here

It is common for human beings to want to be looked at as the victim, while the other person is seen as the guilty party. Everyone likes to be looked at as the correct one. Take a random walk on the street, meet a person who most people look at as bad, chances are he/she actually thinks they are very correct in whatever they do. Making the offender seem like a bad person is one way to gain 'an upper arm' and seem like you are the right person.

In our childhood we often learn that stepping on other people on our way up is not a healthy thing to do. It does not make us much better if we condemn the other person and call them all kinds of names. Obviously, at the moment, we will feel like we are being smothered, but this will only last for a short while.

Justified bitterness

Usually, when someone has done something wrong to us, we feel like we have the right to feel bitter towards them. At that moment it is actually the driving force and we are very liable to being duped into thinking that we are on the right track, yet we are actually headed for a really bad scenario.

In reality, it would help us more to lift ourselves out of that pain, but we let our emotions drive our actions. After a little while, it seems to us like this is actually what we should be feeling – bitterness. So we fail, refuse or simply avoid changing things for the better.

From this point forward, this bitterness is the driving force. It becomes the air we breathe and without it, nothing seems to be in place. However, we are breathing in toxic air and basically harming ourselves in the process. Due to this foul mood, we end up looking at happiness as an alien feeling that we can not even associate with. If bitterness is the driving force, then it's high time we refocused our energy to a new and better driving force.

> *'We are all full of weakness and errors; let us mutually pardon each other our follies'*
>
> -Voltaire

What then needs to be done?

The most important place to begin is by implanting it into your head that stepping on other people on your way up is not healthy. Do not make other people feel down. This may well seem slightly impossible considering you are in the right and you are the victim anyway. However, bear in mind the fact that our whole body is convinced by what our mind thinks. So once you think the other person was really unfair and that you deserve some sort of understanding, you are better off starting afresh.

The risky thing with always blaming the other person is that we will never acknowledge that the same things keep happening over and over again; therefore we will not know how to rise up and put an end to the bad trend.

CHAPTER 2

THE GOOD WE REAP IN FORGIVING SOMEONE

The moment we see beyond our personal desires to be felt sympathy for, we can actually start the journey to that final destination of true forgiveness. A number of scenarios arise that will create pain and will call for forgiveness. There are basically 3 different sets of people who will have wronged us at one point in time. These people who require our forgiveness are apologetic people, unrepentant people and out of reach people. Being able to forgive each of these persons brings along with that forgiveness great advantages.

'Anger makes you smaller, while forgiveness forces you to grow beyond what you were'

- Cherie Carter-Scott

The apologetic person

Quite often, people who we ordinarily see as upright are bound to go wrong and fall off the proverbial rails at some point. Also, those we see as slightly off colour are bound to surprise us and do good for us. In each of these instances, someone may well wrong you and really feel deep inside of them like they should not have done it. They feel remorseful. If someone who wrongs you is apologetic, it is easy to render forgiveness to such a person. Such a person will actually beg for our forgiveness or just make it known that they are apologetic. In such a situation, it does you good to forgive and simply wash away whatever bad memories you have about this person wronging you.

This person will normally gain from your forgiveness too. They know that they were in the wrong and that if you do not forgive them, it's going to haunt them badly and so they will worry about what lies ahead other than what is behind. An apologetic person realises that they have to be forgiven for them to move on well and when you forgive them, they feel like a huge burden has been lifted from their shoulders.

'Forgiveness is me giving up my right to hurt you for hurting me'

- Anonymous

The unrepentant person

There comes a time when someone wrongs you with intent and sometimes is not bothered whether you were rubbed up the wrong way or not. They may not see anything wrong in whatever they did and, therefore, will see no reason to even start asking for forgiveness. Forgiving such a person is simply close to impossible because such a person will typically leave you more bruised than ever before if you tried to forgive them.

People who are unrepentant are bound not even to know that they have done something wrong to you, but you still have to offer them forgiveness just as you would offer it to someone who acknowledges that they are in the wrong. You will reap from the forgiveness a lot more than you expect because it will release you from the bondage of guilt and it will seem like you are releasing a dove out into the free air.

This person who has refused or failed to apologise will also gain, because once you look them in the eyes and forgive them, you are bound to send a very strong message to them that they need to up their game to match yours in terms of forgiveness.

When someone sees the side of you that forgives, irrespective of what the other person does or says, that person will look at you for guidance and it will elevate you. Even if you are not in a position to forgive the person or occurrence outwardly but you do it inwardly, it will change the way you respond to that person as an individual.

Hanging on to the ill feeling is not a good direction to take because it is most likely to create friction and disharmony between you and that person. If you forgive them internally, it does not matter whether you say it to them or you don't; it will simply be visible when you interact with them – you will both be happier.

'Forgiveness is the fragrance that the violet sheds on the heal that has crushed it'

- Mark Twain

The out of reach person

There is a group of people who do you wrong and, for some reason, are untraceable or unreachable for reconciliation. These are often one-off encounters, where you may well not expect to meet this person again.

You may perhaps have bumped into someone on the street and they hurled an insult at you and got you angry but you are sure you will not meet them again. It may perhaps even be someone you have not seen at all; for instance, if someone leaves a poison pen note at your doorstep over something. It may have even been someone you once considered special in a way but have become distant over time.

Such scenarios are rather complicated because the other person is not even aware that you hold something against them. Such a person will not directly get anything good from your forgiveness. However, it does not mean you can not forgive them. If anything, you need to forgive them more because if you harbour any ill feeling towards such a person, it will hurt you more.

You are bound to reap from pardoning such a person no matter whether you see them again or not, or whether they know it or they do not. Everyone around you then is bound to benefit from your forgiveness.

'Never does the human soul appear so strong as when it foregoes revenge, and dares forgive an injury'

- E H Chapin

Here's what to do

Start by letting go of the desire to feel like you are the grieved party and therefore the victim. Forgiveness is something that goes on inside of you, though later you can opt to tell the other person or just keep it within you. To begin forgiving, you need to look inside of yourself and not let anyone distract you from this. Do not inform anyone of your decision just yet. If you take a look back, all those times you played the victim, all the sympathy you got did not exactly make you feel much better; if anything it made you feel much worse. This is simply because sympathy does not tackle the real issue but simply plays with the issue and tosses it back and forth without necessarily helping you to heal. Now that you are aware of what to do about making the correct decision, it is about time you embarked on true healing.

CHAPTER 3

YOUR OWN FORGIVENESS

If there ever was someone who had a control over you, someone who could cause you the greatest pain, someone who could ignore your most necessary requirements and someone for whom forgiveness were truly difficult to render, that person is non other than YOU.

'There is no revenge so complete as forgiveness'
- Josh Billings

Forgiving yourself

Take a walk down memory lane, going as far back as your mind will let you; right from your infant years up to where you are right now. Take a walk through the garden of forgiveness and pick a flower of forgiveness for everything you have ever done. When you get to that time that is now, make a full and total forgiveness of your entire life and smile at the bouquet in your hands, because it truly is beautiful. You are simply naturally inclined to make mistakes just as everyone else is, whether male or female, black or white, young or old. These mistakes are your school of learning, therefore forgiveness is your greatest teacher in this school of learning.

Since you are made of flesh and bones, feelings and emotions, you have all the ability and capacity to do all sorts of undesirable and unhealthy things. You can wrong those you hold dear as well. As a matter of fact, you could currently be feeling hurt because someone did something offensive to you some time back. It may be harder to render forgiveness to yourself than it is to render forgiveness to others. Since only you understand yourself perfectly, there is no way you can settle with pseudo or biased forgiveness.

The risk of self-dislike

If forgiving yourself is something you can not come to terms with, you are only stacking up the pressure from inside. If you have any ill feelings towards yourself, you are not helping yourself at all but only laying the ground for self destruction. It is likely that everything around you will suffer; your relations with other people, your schedule at school, at work, at the gym and everywhere else will be affected.

It could send a signal to those around you that you are okay but you know deep down inside you that things are not okay and it is going to be a short while until everything eventually comes out in the open. Failing to forgive yourself for certain wrongs you committed in the past is bound to create self dislike.

Failing to forgive yourself certainly means that you can not forgive other people. The situation keeps worsening with your heart being punched over and over in the same spot. Before you know it, it will give way and you will begin to think everyone around you feels the same way about you as you feel about yourself – dislike!

In such a situation, loving yourself becomes a huge task. What you feel about yourself determines what others feel about you.

Dislike can lead to self-harm, although that is a far heavier subject than the realms of this book covers, although, certainly, this book will benefit everyone.

Reaping the fruits of self-forgiveness

We are often in line for great things if we practice self-forgiveness. We shall have freed ourselves from all the criticism and we shall be able to notice the real ability that we have within us and we will also start to feel like this is exactly what the true version of us looks like. The moment you cease finding fault with yourself for certain mistakes, then you are headed for better things.

Self-forgiveness has never been and never will be easy. You have no one to pour your heart out to, no one to make a hearty apology to; it's just you in the thick of things and all alone. Self-forgiveness calls for you to search deep down for the strength to forget whatever is in the past and make a decision to move on and become happy.

You can not hide behind anything or tell a lie to yourself. Forgiving yourself requires you to run the whole race. Let bygones be bygones. If you do this, then you are ready to start forgiving others, and only then can you get ready to receive total happiness.

'One thing you will probably remember
well is any time you forgive and forget'

- Franklin P Jones

How to go about it

This time round, you are going to consciously make the determined decision that you deserve all the happiness in the world. This is an entitlement to you and only you.

Other people may well not find it relevant that you have forgiven yourself, but you need to know that it is not for them anyway. Everything at the moment is wholly about you. You are trying to search for healing for yourself. It is only you who can control what happens in your life and right now, you are tasked with making a choice over whether you want to heal by letting go of your past or get sucked up in un-ending pain.

CHAPTER 4

RECONCILIATION AFTER FORGIVENESS

Forgiving people

Forgiving other people en masse makes the whole process of forgiveness a lot easier. You could opt to make lists of groups of *unknowns*, *buddies*, *relatives*, *the deep pain causers* and *all the rest*. There is no problem in adding some other groups for instance: *former lovers*, *neighbours*, *colleagues* and *workers*. However, there should be one of true humanity, and that is from the heart. You can work through the list, forgiving each group, one at a time. When you realise the good in forgiving, you will be ready and willing to forgive others too.

Being forgiven

Within your own conscience, play out a scenario and actually seek out forgiveness from those you may well have rubbed up the wrong way. You may be shocked to learn that, actually, many people do want to forgive you. Therefore, give them the chance to practice their forgiveness.

Certain people are not good with accepting apologies and so may well put you down with seething words even after you have apologised. So be sure to do it with caution. First play out the whole thing within your mind before you put it to practice, and then decide when you are going to do it for real and go for it.

Degrees of forgiveness

If you looked at how much you can forgive those who hurt you, how much would you say you can forgive them on a scale of 1 to 10 (10 being the maximum amount of forgiveness)? Maybe 2? Perhaps 4? Probably even 10!

Well, you may perhaps want to know that forgiveness is not about having it all your own way. You can start small with an ultimate target of eventually hitting the 10 mark, but stick to reality. Someone who hurt you badly may well not be easy to forgive to the maximum of 10. No worries. Go slow, bit by bit, until such a time when you can actually forgive them wholly. Begin from wherever you can manage and increase the score while targeting the maximum forgiveness rate of 10.

Forgiveness of people and occurrences

Forgiving someone is totally different from forgiving what they did. So what do you do? It is better and more workable to forgive the events and actions as you remember them. As each occurrence comes to mind, keep forgiving what everyone did.

'To err is human; to forgive, divine'

- Alexander Pope

So now you have forgiven this person, perhaps wondering what should happen next. It hurt you so bad but, somehow, you managed to look within yourself for the energy and will to forgive them and perhaps you have managed to do that. But you are still wondering – *will this now bring us back together?*

Well, not exactly. Being able to reconcile with someone is a long process and forgiveness is just a part of the long journey. You may well have the most noble of reasons to forgive and the most pure of hearts to let go of the past, but the fact is that reconciliation is something that is never done alone.

Resolution as a brainchild of forgiveness

The idea of reconciliation is sometimes not an easy decision to deal with. It mostly depends on a particular trend of events that is scheduled and timed. You may well be ready to forgive while the other person is not yet ready to get involved in forgiveness at all, whether to receive it or to give it. That does not matter. It is your time to forgive – NOW.

Most times, forgiveness is a prerequisite for a resolution of reconciliation. As earlier discussed, the person who has wronged is normally repentant and in such cases they will show that they are sorry and would like to be forgiven. In the event that you take heed and actually offer them forgiveness from the bottom of your heart, reconciliation will almost be inevitable. A broken and mended relationship turns out to be stronger than one that has never been broken, almost like how bones can become even stronger once broken and then healed.

Unable to create resolution

It is so sad that, many times, we are ready to forgive and yet the other person is not yet in a position to welcome our forgiveness. Many times, someone offends you and they are not in the least bit even sorry or apologetic. With such a person, reconciliation is almost impossible.

If someone is not at all sorry, that means they are not yet in a position to venture into reconciliation. They may perhaps require that you give them a little more time to look at the situation with more perspective and probably realise where and how exactly they went wrong. In such cases, forgiveness is hard but when you do it, reconciliation is just around the corner.

It is not really a sure deal that forgiveness automatically mends all broken links. However, you are working hard to make sure that between you and the other person there is less and less resentment. It is for sure that once you forgive, you are safely on the road to reconciliation.

The absence of the person during the time of forgiveness will render the reconciliation unattainable, at least for the moment. It is however important that you wipe out any ill feelings from within your heart. True, things may well not get back to how they were, but the sad feelings and bad memories can be wiped away and replaced with the former nice and sweet memories that you both once shared.

'Yes, this is what good is: to forgive evil. There is no other good'

- Antonio Porchia

The way forward

You, unlike the other person, can be ready whenever you want to. Being able to forgive does not entail you just turning a blind eye to the wrong that the other person has done to you; neither does it make what they did any better. Therefore you may actually offer the other person forgiveness without necessarily condoning what they did. Forgiving them will lift the weight from your heart and soul and you will be happier once again.

Remember, it is up to you to decide whether you initially forgive the person wholly or just for the act of what they did. Take it step by step.

CHAPTER 5

WHEN DOES FORGIVENESS LEAD TO RESOLUTION?

Assuming you are still lost in thought about when exactly you should forgive someone, well, the time is NOW. At the time when you are thinking more clearly and you can judge the situation more sanely, then it is time that you carry this forward.

'Forgiving is love's toughest work, and love's biggest risk. If you twist it into something it was never meant to be, it can make you a doormat or an insufferable manipulator. Forgiving seems almost unnatural. Our sense of fairness tells us people should pay for the wrong they do. But forgiving is love's power to break nature's rule.'

- Lewis B Smedes

This, however, should not be mistaken to mean that to forgive someone you have to wait until you are in the mood to forgive – the mood may perhaps take forever to come! Then what? Feel resentment for someone for your whole life?

In the event that the person who wronged you is someone you hold dear, it is worthwhile to forgive them because your resolution with this person is dependant on the forgiveness. However, the person who wronged you may perhaps not be present or may possibly simply be unreachable. Sometimes, reconciling with the person may not be the right thing to do, especially if it involved some sort of assault or physical attack. In such cases, reconciliation may well be a little less possible, but forgiveness is attainable.

Being hurt by someone very close and dear to you will create you great pain. Once you think deeply about it and refuse to let bygones be bygones, there is a worry that you are bound to start feeling very bad feelings towards this person and if you are not careful, it can easily graduate into a more distasteful scenario where you actually cannot stand this person.

Failure or refusal to forgive can leave a lasting impression on your life as it will drag itself into each and every situation in your life. Before you know it; your whole life will be full of a lot of sad feelings and ill will towards almost every person and situation. With time, you are bound to fail to enjoy your life and thus live a miserable and unhappy life.

Your forgiveness of someone should be out of your sentiments or feelings. As a matter of fact, how you feel will mostly make you think you can not or should not forgive someone. After all, you are feeling the way you are simply because this person hurt you and you felt you needed to act and play the victim but for some reason your heart is still not at rest.

Every person has at some point made a mistake, and this person is no exception. Why hold a grudge against them when, in all honesty, you are still in great shape, fully alive and well, not seriously hurt or injured and you too have hurt a number of people in the past? It is time to do unto them what you would want them to do unto you.

The acceptance within yourself that forgiveness is the way forward will open up an unforgettable healing journey for you – try it and see.

Willingness?

You could have been told that you need time to relax to allow yourself to be angry because it will help you release the pain. However, just sit back and ask yourself a simple question – "What if everyone let themselves be angry whenever they felt like it. Would we be able to live with one another in this world?"

If you give yourself time to be angry you run the risk of actually desiring to remain in the state of an offended party, basking in the sympathy and attention. However, there are specific times that you should be angry, which is touched upon in this book.

The truth is, forgiveness is a very difficult thing to do, particularly if someone does not show any remorse and is bent on refusing to admit that they are in the wrong.

If you are confused and do not know what to do, it will help if you write things down in some notebook or simply try to think deeply or, better still, meditate. Writing things down this way is called journaling, and it's the next best thing to talking to someone or if what you are writing is not for anyone's ears.

Talking about it is the best way to clearing the air, so this could be a time when you need someone you can trust to talk to and pour your heart out to. This is also the time when you may well need to think back to those times when you were the one in the wrong and when you were forgiven by others.

It is also important to note that once you forgive, you are on course to feel better, have more peace and generally gain more accolades in the eyes of the forgiven party.

There is great need to be ready, both inside and outside, when it comes to the time for forgiveness. Do not dwell on the wrong and on trivial issues. Forgiveness gives you better results if you do it when you still feel the pain. Because afterwards it is hard to shift the resentment and pain in order to start the healing process of forgiving.

Being resentful and cold towards someone at this point in time is the last thing you should be doing because it is going to take away a part of you, both internally and externally.

Obviously you will not be expected to burst into someone's presence and just scream out, "You are forgiven!" You have to go about it in a more mature and composed manner. Things do not occur in a flash. They are gradual.

Before you can finally let it go, distance yourself from the occurrence that caused your hurt. Distancing yourself from some painful event is probably the ignition for the process of forgiveness. If you continue reading, you will learn that forgiveness is not simply a single act, it is a full process.

Being around the wrongdoer

You may possibly find it rather difficult and very demanding to have to be in the vicinity of the person who hurt you. It is totally up to you to make up your mind whether to show up at certain events or not. It is at such times that you have to make a conscious decision to do what you think is the right thing to do. In the event that you show up at certain events, you should expect some uncomfortable situations where you may well even feel totally out of place. However, it is very important for you to keep a clear mind because it is at these events that you could get some much needed strategies to help you in your process of forgiveness.

Forgiveness and Love Conquers All

Forgiveness is yours

The purpose of forgiveness is not to make sure that someone ends up changing into what you expect them to be, as this is dominance. The purpose is actually to make your own life better, more worthy and less stressful. Forgiveness reduces the hold that the wrongdoer has over you and empowers you.

Forgiveness now

In the past, people always looked at the future as hopeless and totally bleak, so they opted to look at things in only the present vein. This therefore meant that they thought less about the future and ended up wasting away the present. The problem with this is that it leaves you totally clueless about what lies ahead. It is impossible to know what lies ahead of us so we have no idea what we are missing when we decide to cling on to all of the anger. Another second of anger could eliminate any chances of reconciliation.

'Forgiveness is the answer to the child's dream of a miracle by which what is broke is made whole again, what is soiled is made clean again.'

- Dag Hammarskjold

Plan of action

It is of no use for you to keep postponing the act of forgiveness because the time for you to forgive is NOW.

1. What you need to do is sit down and observe the importance of forgiving as well as how the scenario you are now experiencing has caused change in your feelings, attitudes and way of life.

2. As soon as you are geared up and ready for the forgiveness, let go of whatever it is that is bothering you.
3. Stop looking at yourself as the offended person and stop letting the other person control you in any way.
4. Do not look at yourself as someone who has been hurt, and in releasing victimship you will find there is a chance that you may well realise how warm, sympathetic and considerate you can be.

CHAPTER 6

ACCOMPLISHING TRUE FORGIVENESS

You can not sit back and hope that forgiveness comes over you and that it just happens in an epiphany. Simply mentioning with lip service that you have forgiven someone is not sufficient. Being able to forgive is a lot more than simply stating the words. It goes deeper than that. Forgiving is a way of life.

'We are told that people stay in love because of chemistry, or because they remain intrigued with each other, because of many kindnesses, because of luck . . . But part of it has got to be forgiveness and gratefulness.'

- Ellen Goodman

By absorbing this material you are a step closer to knowing exactly what forgiveness is all about. If you properly internalise the ideas and notions set out in this book, you are bound to grasp the real meaning of forgiveness. If you constantly practice forgiveness, it will become second nature to you and it will come naturally.

Cathartic bitterness

A great many experts say that prior to forgiveness, it is important for someone to feel a sense of bitterness towards the offender. Find someone you trust and let them know exactly how you feel about your situation. Before you forgive someone, there is a need for you to fully accept the situation and embrace it. Experts insist that you need to sit down and let your *self* feel the pain that you should be feeling. If in anyway you try to ignore it, you are bound to slow the process of healing. This is not to say that you should bathe in victimship!

Rewriting the scenario

When you have expressed yourself to those around you that you trust, search for the good points in the scenario that you have gone through. For instance, it could occur that the scenario you just went through just made you more resilient or courageous. The best way to rewrite the whole scenario is by re-editing the version of the story that you tell other people concerning how you were wronged. Cease to look at yourself as the offended person and start to think of yourself as someone who has overcome a really tough situation – a brave person.

The aim is to remember all the aspects of what just happened without having to feel very irate about it. It is important to reflect on what people have done to us so that in the future we can avoid any such similar occurrences in our lives.

'Forgiveness is a virtue of the brave'

- Indira Gandhi

A simple survival strategy

Here is a simple survival strategy that is going to help you and will not take too much of your time. It will take no more than half a minute and will help you a lot. You can do it hourly throughout the day or as required.

Take in some air with your nose and let that air settle into your belly, then exhale it and let your belly get smaller. This is called 'belly breathing'. Do this the first time, second time, and then on the third time create an image of somebody you hold dearly, somebody who makes you happy, or just think of some really nice place.

In the process of trying to analyse this image, keep taking deep breaths while trying to come up with ways to let the offence play out in your mind without necessarily holding any ill feelings towards the person. Continue looking at the nice image that you have created in your mind.

The journey of forgiveness in 7 steps

1. Recognise the mistake

When beginning the journey of forgiveness, you have to begin by observing that something wrong has been done and therefore it calls for forgiveness. As you read on, you will realise that this book explains why it is not helpful to just brush it aside. Your bitterness and anger towards someone will keep you in perpetual unhappiness if you just brush the issue aside.

2. Know that forgiveness is necessary

Sometimes we can be sucked into the other person's desire to be offered forgiveness, but the truth is we need to render the forgiveness a lot more than the other person needs us to offer it. All the resentment that lies in your heart is simply causing damage to you mostly.

3. Stop pointing the finger of guilt

Totally forgiveness does not have any room for finding fault with someone. It is very difficult to find fault with someone and then go ahead to say you are forgiving them fully. Someone who forgives forgets the wrongs.

4. Ill will can make you ill
Failure and refusal to forgive brings on us a lot of unworthy and unwanted feelings which make us think and feel badly towards those who have hurt us. The journey of happiness will be a lot more bearable if you let go of all the ill will.

5. Openness and honesty is important
It is useless to fake forgiveness and it is even more useless to push yourself to forgive without the will to do so. Saying the words is one thing, meaning them is another.

Just because someone wakes up one morning and says, "Today I am going to be rich," does not automatically make them rich.

6. Do not look back
After the forgiveness, try not to keep a memory of the things that were done against you. Let go of the situation that you have just forgiven, because only then will your heart be freed.

7. Claim forgiveness and start afresh
If you genuinely know that you have wronged someone, it is worthwhile to come clean that you are wrong and go ahead and apologise. Be remorseful and show regret for what you have done.

Ask for their forgiveness and do not try to find reasons to justify what you did. It is also important to know that someone who is going to forgive you needs to do so without being pressured in any way. Just do your part of repentance and leave the rest to them.

Forgiveness and Love Conquers All

To offer an excuse for what you have done after seeking forgiveness is simply a way of trying to deflect it, and the aggrieved party will sense this sooner or later.

Often an unequivocal acceptance that you were wrong by a simple request for forgiveness is far more impacting than that of a whole diatribe of why you did what you did.

The first rule of when you find you have dug yourself into a hole is to stop digging. Digging yourself deeper into trouble will take far longer to get out of, so just seek simple forgiveness, but do not be surprised if the initial request is rebuked, as they too are going through pain and may well need the night to sleep on before it dawns on them that the heat of the moment has passed, and it's a new day.

Remember, seeking forgiveness must come from the heart and be real, and it is also a learning period for you too. To seek forgiveness with crocodile tears is not a learning experience and you will simply go on to commit more and more hurt, and before you know it, you will not know the meaning of forgiveness! If this happens then there are far deeper consequences and by no means is it something that is easy to counter or remedy.

'Forgiveness is the final form of love'

-Reinhold Niebuhr

Plan of action

Forgiveness is not something you should start tomorrow or later during the day. I have to stress this, as it is the mainstay of how it works best - start it right NOW! Begin getting yourself into the growth pattern of forgiving people. Begin with the smallest of circumstances and work your way up. Also, start with the ones closest to you – the ones you love.

Do not allow your sad past to rule your present situation. Someone may, perhaps, have said something bad to you yesterday evening, but today they cracked a joke and made you smile.

Once you realise that you are re-living a certain bad memory, focus your mind on forgiving that person and evaluate what may perhaps happen if you forgive them. After a while you will get used to forgiving and it will be part and parcel of you and something that comes from your heart.

CHAPTER 7

TRUE FORGIVENESS – HOW TO IDENTIFY IT

Being able to fully render forgiveness to someone is something that has deep and far reaching positive effects, both within you and even on the outside. However, before you get to that point of forgiveness, there is a need to be critical and observant about other peoples' invisible pain.

'One forgives to the degree that one loves'
-Francois de La Rochefoucauld

Many people are really inconsiderate and will not even show any emotion during times of forgiveness. However, we can not entirely blame such people; we are different after all. Everybody tries to live their lives the best way they think they can, depending on how they were brought up. Therefore the onus is upon you to begin accepting people entirely without wanting them to change who they truly are just to suit your expectations.

The idea of forgiveness should not be mistaken to be some sort of magic wand that will automatically wipe away everything. There comes a time when someone may well wonder whether they are on the right course anyway.

You may perhaps not exactly see anything on the outside that shows signs of forgiveness, but there are some indicators of honest and genuine forgiveness.

For us to be able to understand how to even think positively about someone who has wronged us, we need to begin by bearing in mind the fact that all people try to look for ways to make themselves happy. In an attempt to seek their happiness, the wrongdoer mistakenly stepped on our toes and so should be looked at as an innocent attempt to acquire happiness at our expense.

So now the question still lingers in the air – if true and honest forgiveness will free someone from all the bitterness, why don't people forgive a lot more often? The answer is simply – because forgiving is simply difficult! Apart from that, we aren't well clued on how exactly to go about it and many times we are afraid that if we forgave someone, they could take things for granted and do the same wrong thing to us again simply because they think we were not offended in the first place.

Journaling forgiveness

Remember what I mentioned about journaling, take some time and write down a note of forgiveness. It may well not be that you will send it to the party concerned, just to try and go over what happened, how it impacted on you, your expectations, and then at the end, make it clear that you forgive them wholeheartedly and honestly.

Take time and write down another note, but this time an apology. Try to put yourself in their shoes and think up something you would say, how you would feel and how you would respond, then write it down.

Divest yourself of self-chastisement

When we do something wrong to someone, we usually begin to feel a sense of 'guilt' which can prompt us to use that feeling to propel us forward to wanting to be acquitted of our wrongdoing. On the other hand, if another person has done something bad to us, we carry on expecting some sort of compensation from them for the wrong done to us. So now, as briefly explained earlier, you know why at times it is tough to secure forgiveness.

However, simply having this feeling of guilt will not bring about forgiveness. In the same vein, another person can not initiate the forgiveness; it has to come from us.

All in all, failure to let go of the past will only keep us stuck in the circumstance and we will be bound by those previous happenings.

If we look at the past as very bad, there is a worry that we shall remain frozen in it, or at least our persona will. What is in the past is in the past and the only thing we can do about the past is pick a leaf from it. We need to study and learn from it rather than sit back and sulk about what happened. When you forgive, you will be freed of any uncertainty and you will find yourself getting better and stronger.

Being able to render our own selves forgiveness requires us to look at past experiences and pick out lessons from them.

Healing the wound

Normally, after forgiveness, there is mutual agreement to forget the past and a renewal of the bond between two people. Once you can sit down and see you and the other party returning back to the good old ways after the forgiveness, then after all, you are, surely, truly a forgiver.

The bond between you and that person may well not be re-fixed, no worries. For all you know, the other person may perhaps not be remorseful or may well not even be accessible. When a bond is broken, both parties have to be a part of the re-fixing of it, even though it requires only one to render the forgiveness. What goes on at your end should not be determined by what goes on at the other person's end. Sometimes you could offer forgiveness but the other person is not ready or willing to get the bond that you share back in repair.

Litmus paper for forgiveness

You can actually apply a test to yourself to ascertain if you have truly forgiven someone. When you forgive someone genuinely, you should be able to let go of whatever happened and start to feel like whatever wrong was done is really insignificant and may well not even have happened anyway. In the event that you are constantly reminding yourself of the wrong, then you are not entirely there yet in terms of forgiveness. That is the litmus paper test.

When you realise that this is what you are going through, do not throw a tantrum or get worried, you are on course to finally complete the cycle of forgiveness. You may well have forgiven the person and even made up with them, but somehow you still feel angered or somewhat bitter towards them, just give it some time. The ill feelings that you are holding will slowly fade.

However, do not be misguided to think that these ill feelings will be washed away automatically even without you doing anything about them. There is a need to keep pondering over the issue of forgiveness until such a time when you can actually picture the person as not having wronged you at all. Forgiveness is something that requires your involvement.

At the end of the day, this is your litmus paper test for whether your forgiveness is real or not real. Eventually you will realise that you can now focus your energy and commitment to other things that will help you build your bond with other people.

Try to visualise them as nice people and look at the good things that exist between the two of you.

There could be many other issues that determine whether or not your bond with this person is re-fixed, but that should not stop you from acting like you have truly and fully forgiven the person.

Run the scenario of forgiveness through your mind, allow yourself to view it as a mini mind movie if it helps. See yourself as the star in the movie, and isn't it usually the hero in the movie that is the one that has the magnanimity to forgive before anyone else? Alright, we are not talking about *Rambo* series of films here, they are works of fiction... We are talking about just plain honest to goodness movies without the dramatics – try it, be the star.

'We are all on a life long journey and the core of its meaning, the terrible demand of its centrality is forgiving and being forgiven.'

-Martha Kilpatrick

Plan of action

Take a look at the situation – does it feel like you have finally let things go? Okay, well at least you are part of the way there.

1. Look at what is happening currently. Try to take deep breaths and let each breath out represent the sadness and bitterness going out of you and every breath in is a new energy, a new happiness and joy, a new beginning altogether.

2. Let your mind be free and relaxed and let it dwell on sympathy and kindness.
3. Look at the other person as, perhaps, an ignorant person who does not know they are even hurting others and does so not because he or she really intends to.
4. The moment you have some consideration for this person, then you will be more in harmony and tranquillity will sweep over the whole of your being.

CHAPTER 8

THE WRONGDOER IS STUBBORN, WHAT NEXT?

Forgiveness is something you only have partial control over. There are certain things you just can not direct or steer. In the process of forgiveness, you can only control your own actions and decisions. It is unrealistic to expect someone to do exactly what you want, therefore you may well have offered them forgiveness but they are not warming to the idea of it or they may perhaps not really seem to be changing.

'Nobody forgets where he buried the hatchet'
- Frank McKinney

When you offer forgiveness to someone, it is common that something about them changes. Someone who is remorseful and truly sorry for what they have done will appreciate and welcome the forgiveness with open arms. They will also try to make it a point to keep away from wronging you again. As much as this is desired, it does not always happen and should not in any way affect the forgiveness.

Dangerous bonds

Someone may possibly require your forgiveness but for some reason they are cold, unwelcoming and very negative towards you. This does not change the fact that you already forgave what they did. Do not allow their actions and words to make you regret your decision to forgive them. The moment you feel any regret, then you have not entirely forgiven this person.

Someone may keep doing something that you clearly do not like. You have to look at what bond you have with that person, and depending on the depth of that bond it may possibly be recommended that you keep away from such a person. If you decide to keep away from this person, you should still hold on to the forgiveness otherwise anger and ill will can be a part of you, even when you and that person are no longer in touch.

Forgive and go

At the end of the day, the behaviour of people and the way they act is not in any way a part of what your impression about forgiveness is. Do the forgiveness and carry on going forward. Leave the worrying to the other person. Eat what is on your plate and leave the rest to them.

Begin every day with some encouraging words and statements. Convince yourself about the strength you have to deal with whatever situation comes your way. Having optimism is a very important thing in life; without it we are simply hopeless.

Be sure to have optimism and faith in what lies ahead for you. Once you think with optimism, you are bound to live your life with more ease and relaxation. Being joyous or happy is not something you should feel guilty about.

Give love to yourself as well as to those around you. By doing this, you are bound to be happier as time progresses.

The keyword of 'love' is not to be knocked, as that is where the majority of spiritual healing starts.

Forgiveness and Love Conquers All

'Not to forgive is to be imprisoned by the past, by old grievances that do not permit life to proceed with new business. Not to forgive is to yield oneself to another's control... to be locked into a sequence of act and response, of outrage and revenge, tit for tat, escalating always. The present is endlessly overwhelmed and devoured by the past. Forgiveness frees the forgiver. It extracts the forgiver from someone else's nightmare.'

- Lance Morrow

Plan of action

1. Play your role of forgiver and leave the other person to play their role as well. Taking a quote from one of the character's in a Shakespeare play gives more depth to this meaning that we all have roles to play:

   All the world's a stage,
   And all the men and women merely players;
   They have their exits and their entrances,
   And one man in his time plays many parts,
   His acts being seven ages.

2. Look at your feelings and attitudes towards this person and the situation. You may well easily claim that the person just rubs you the wrong way always or that they make you mad all the time, but you need to look at the situation a little more closely and identify what exactly it is that makes you mad.
3. You may well always feel angry when your partner lays the table in a certain manner or your colleague uses a certain screen saver on his/her

office computer. However, you have to look at the root of the anger to ascertain the background of the whole issue. It may perhaps not work all the time, but at least give it a try on one occasion and try and see what you can do to change things.

4. It may require you to ask the person to change, and then maybe it is high time you simply tried to accept the person the way they are.
5. As hard as it may be, try to look at the good aspects about that person. If it is very unbearable, try to avoid crossing paths with this person.

CHAPTER 9

SEEKING FORGIVENESS

Many schools of thought contend that forgiving ourselves is a way of absolving ourselves from certain bad things we have done without having to worry about being answerable in any way. Nothing could be so further from the truth. As a matter of fact, the opposite is true – forgiving yourself is the beginning of something good in your life. It is the gateway to avoiding living a lie.

'There's no point in burying a hatchet if you're going to put up a marker on the site'
- Sydney Harris

Forgiving yourself is the one thing that will maintain your strength in life. A person who forgives him/herself is not someone who is individualistic or selfish. Someone who keeps thinking that they are in the wrong and can do nothing about it is more likely to be personal, selfish and individualistic.

There comes a time, however, when you are the one who is seeking forgiveness. At times we are offended by the behaviour of others when people do wrong to us; however there are times when we are the ones in the wrong.

Although it may, at times, seem rather a rare thing and something that is not really done these days, the truth is that if you have wronged someone then you should go ahead and ask for forgiveness.

Telling someone you are 'sorry' is very different from actually seeking forgiveness from that person. It requires that you go one step further and acknowledge that you were wrong or that you are truly remorseful.

Here are a few examples:

- "If I were you, I would be mad too, but please forgive me."
- "I know I did something very bad, please excuse it and give me forgiveness."
- "You must be hurting right now, I pray you forgive me."

These statements above will tear through any rock of anger or ill will. Someone who understands will not turn down such an apology, especially since it is rare for people to ask for forgiveness.

Obviously anyone will be taken aback by such statements. In most cases the wonderful surprise will prompt them to forgive you from deep down. Once you incorporate this into your daily life, it almost always comes automatically that you are ready to forgive and that you will receive genuine forgiveness.

In the event that you are the one seeking forgiveness, there is no way you can rush the other person to forgive you. There is no point in seeking this simply because you think you are required to do it.

Forgiveness depends on how genuine and earnest the appeal is. As mentioned earlier, someone who is hurt will very easily tell that you are being plastic or pretentious about your request for forgiveness. In such cases, it will create a lot more damage than already caused. Once you get used to seeking forgiveness from other people, you will create an impression about you that other people will admire. Other people will want to associate with you and you too will find it easier to start offering forgiveness to those who wronged them because you will have shown them how to go about the issue of forgiveness.

Getting this practice into your everyday life will help you get in sync more and more with forgiveness and you will understand everything about forgiveness both from the end of the forgiver and the wrongdoer.

'*To forgive is the highest, most beautiful form of love. In return, you will receive untold peace and happiness.'*

– Robert Muller

Plan of action

Pose a question to the other person, "Will you forgive me – please?" Make sure you jot down responses to questions like:

i) How must I forgive?
ii) If I forgive, will I benefit anything?
iii) Is there any advantage of this forgiveness?
iv) Are there any lessons I have learned?
v) After I forgive, what will my life be like?

Forgiving yourself sometimes helps people get over the problems that come with procrastination and also helps to create a positive change in how someone acts. Forgiving oneself for procrastination will typically help someone eliminate ill feelings they may be harbouring.

Pick out a list of 3 things that you can offer forgiveness to yourself for. Jot down a forgiveness note for each of the 3 things and then make sure your name is signed on it so as to affirm this to yourself.

1. Take the blame and shoulder it.
2. Be remorseful and truly seek forgiveness.
3. Forgive yourself and stop blaming yourself.

CHAPTER 10

RELEASE THE PAST AND SECURE FREEDOM

It is so sad, yet so true that what happens in our lives can become a part and parcel of our lives and may possibly not want to leave us. It is, however, very crucial and important that we drop any attachments we have with the past sad events, bad memories, wrongdoings, errors and shortcomings.

'It's easier to ask forgiveness than it is to get permission'
- Grace Hopper

We can let go of the past by simply looking at the positive things in the situations we looked at as bad. The moment we turn these bad historical events into learning experiences and pick out lessons from them, we are basically on the right course to break ourselves free form the hurt linked with these events.

How to let go of the past

The most basic method one can use to let go of the past is by looking at it as a learning experience. If a particular scenario from history keeps popping up, and for some reason it brings with it a lot of painful memories, then this is an indication that there is a lot of unsorted business within us – not with any other person or with any other situation. It may well be that someone wronged us, it may well be that we wronged someone. Probably we did something regrettable at a time when we were very vulnerable. It is impossible to change the past, therefore we have to find a way to generate some lessons from the experiences we went through. If we are able to look at our history and think of it as a learning experience, then we are heading in the right direction.

Remaining stuck in history will block our view of the future and we will end up washing away our dreams. When we get hurt, it happens in a number of ways:

1. Hurt we bring upon ourselves
2. Conscious hurt
3. Hurt from the past

The hurt we bring upon ourselves

The hurt we bring upon ourselves usually comes from our historical errors and shortcomings. The errors and shortcomings are not exactly causing the discomfort; it is the knowledge of the fact that we can not render forgiveness to ourselves for these mistakes. In the event that an error you made is haunting you, there is a need for you to offer yourself forgiveness.

It is common knowledge that you can not undo what has been done. We are not judged or determined by what our past holds; we are judged by what we are *right now* and where we are. Stop blaming yourself for past failures.

Mindful pain

The mindful pain we carry around with us on a day to day basis is simply the anguish that we are not even sure about it. Consciously, the pain is something that happened some time back. It made you angry and, somehow, you have never stopped being angry. In many cases these mindful pains are more easily identifiable and they can make you seem like you can not get over a certain grudge. Obviously, forgiving someone is the one and only shortcut to happiness.

Pain from the past

Pain from the past is often difficult to analyse and remedy. On some occasions, something may well happen and we don't know that it has far-reaching effects. The particular occurrence could have happened a very long time ago but the effects still exist. If someone's childhood was full of deprivation or torment of some sort, they will have a certain phase of their lives where they will keep dashing back to their childhood experiences.

Sometimes people become angry due to past trauma or events caused by the wrongdoer. Once the wrongdoing has been forgiven, that is when forgiveness will sum it all up by helping you let go of what is causing you the unhappiness.

Each and every wrongdoing against you is likely to cause a frozen persona of your psyche to be frozen in that time zone. Thus if you have myriads of frozen personas spread over a long period of time going back years, then of course there is a lot of work to do, it all depends how far back you want to go in unlocking those frozen personas.

When I was a practicing clinical hypnotherapist I used to use an open-eyed hypnosis technique for unlocking those personas in clients I worked with. This was a successful way of empowering the client's persona to move forward, but without the client actually experiencing any of the trauma of whatever it was I was dealing with.

This technique I used was formulated by a man called David Grove; consequently it was called Groverian Therapy. If you ever get the opportunity to experience such a therapy then do take advantage of it, as it is the only therapeutic technique I have come across that is able to go back (T [trauma] -1) to the second just before the trauma and then build a bridge over it and to come out safely just one second in time after the trauma (T [trauma] +1), and all without any regression taking place!

I incorporate some of those methods, albeit of my own design, in some of my therapeutic audios, details of which can be found at the end of this book.

'Forgive all who have offended you,
not for them, but for yourself'

- Harriet Nelson

Plan of action

1. Let your mind move around freely and identify the different situations in which you need to forgive.
2. Look at the situation that critically calls for forgiveness. Move your mind to just before the event and think about how you felt before this situation showed up.
3. Think of all the people who have wronged you and recall what bond you shared with them prior to the wrongdoing. Try and rebuild this bond.
4. Live through the situation and remember the happier times just before the situation. Once you do that, then you can now walk through the pain, making sure you recall as much as you can about it. See how the pain has shifted over time.

5. Take a look at the results. Think about what you are missing, how bad the bond is now, how much disappointment has been caused and so on.
6. Be sure to journal this in writing and also put down anything else that happened in terms of changes.
7. Did your regard for this person diminish? Did your opinion about them change? Is there something about you that was affected by the situation but you would like to reinstate?
8. After you have insightfully looked at the situation and gone through all the memories, then turn to your current situation and try to create an explanation for why events occurred the way they did.
9. Study all the people who are involved and study how each person contributed to what is happening. You may perhaps realise that you have a lot of contribution to it yourself. Probably you ignored reconciliation at the time or you thought what was happening was well deserved.
10. Do not get sucked in to the vacuum by self-reproach or apportioning blame.
11. Do not create any excuses or try to vindicate anything. You have to be able to forgive yourself too.
12. Do not try to create an explanation for the wrong things that the other person did to you.
13. Forgiving and excusing are two very separated and different things.
14. You could excuse a teenager who worries a lot about how they fit in with other people and you could forgive someone who uses foul language.

Take as much time as possible to consider what exactly happened.

CHAPTER 11

FORGIVENESS AS A RELEASING TOOL

At this point in time you are in a better position to judge events. You have made an assessment of the whole situation. The question that you should be asking yourself now is, "Am I truly forgiven?"

Humanity is quite complex. So complex that many times we get sucked up in ill will towards people and when we feel this way for a long time, it becomes a part of who we are. We cannot function properly without these rather undesirable feelings.

'He who cannot forgive breaks the bridge over which he himself must pass'

- George Herbert

A part of us always wants impartiality. Rendering forgiveness to someone amidst sadness and, worse still, when the other person is, somehow, out of reach or not ready to indulge will typically create great disappointment. We could possibly feel that such people should not even be considered for forgiveness.

You do not forgive someone simply because you are obliged to or because it is morally correct. You do it because it is what is good for you. Our purpose, for us all, is a happy and fulfilling life, forgiveness helps us attain this.

Forgiving surges you to the fore of a happy life.

Failure to forgive will keep you locked in a situation that you have no control over. Therefore being able to forgive is the only way you are bound to free your rather imprisoned heart.

Journal the impact that forgiveness is bound to have on your life. Imagine all the benefits. You will realise that the sacrifices you have to make are actually very few compared to the benefits. Moving on in life requires that you are free at heart, forgiveness gives you this freedom.

Human beings are often overwhelmed with anger and bitterness or resentment. Our feelings may be uncontrollable, but our dislike of things and places can be controlled. The issue of resentment possesses us so much, but we tend to ignore or fail to realise its true meaning or impact and we even fail to describe or identify it.

Bitterness

As we begin to discover what it truly is and how it affects us, it is worthwhile to look at the issue of bitterness in depth. It is an attitude or experience where someone is irate or furious over a situation, assumed or real, that made them feel hurt. Having bitterness towards someone will automatically render all your relationships with other people shaky because it has far-reaching effects. Issues of bitterness can be looked at in different perspectives: hidden, exposed or belated.

In some instances, resentment is very visible. One may dislike a colleague who rides on another person's success. One may also feel resentment towards an old flame's new partner or a neighbour's successful son. A host of things are responsible for creating resentment amongst people.

There are times when we least expect it, but resentment finds its way to our hearts. The important thing is our relationships with other people. If we keep feeling any anger towards someone, over and over, it will only keep multiplying, therefore the most logical solution is to dispel it as soon as possible. By doing this you are making your job of forgiveness much easier.

Resolving bitterness

Forgiveness is the solution to bitterness. If you are bitter with someone for one reason or another, you are only going to be freed from that bitterness by actually forgiving that person. Bitterness that presents itself openly is easier to deal with as long as you realise that it is important to render forgiveness to the person that you feel bitter with.

The unexposed and covered bitterness is trickier than the others. Bitterness is the major reason why people fail to attain any kind of happiness for themselves. Open resentment or anger will not silently eat us up as much as bitterness will.

Since it is more elusive and difficult to notice, many people tend to have a lot of bitterness bottled up inside of them without even knowing that they are in the red zone. As soon as something triggers off any ill will, all the 'stored' bitterness is released and this affects any attempts at reconciliation with some, only worsening the already dire situation.

In case bitterness is not sorted out early, there is a worry that bitterness will still remain hidden even after there is apparent resolution of a conflict. This hidden or unexposed bitterness is a huge threat to well-being and general happiness.

First of all, it is important to observe that something is wrong, thus work towards letting go of all the ill will.

Usually, this covered or unexposed emotion will be seen through: loss of trust, doubting intentions and anger.

A person sticking to bitterness tends to lose trust in someone and they may not even be aware of it. Sometimes it could even be in circumstances that are not even remotely connected to the particular situation in question.

Scenario

Look at a situation between two friends; Cathy and Bridget argue about who exactly used up Cathy's last remaining lotion. After a heated argument they come to a conclusion and even say "sorry" to one another. Apparently the situation is now settled.

However, Cathy may well still feel the resentment because she feels that Bridget actually used up her lotion but is refusing to admit to it. This could make the resentment carry on to other issues.

With time, Cathy could think that Bridget is not exactly fair when it comes to cleaning around the house they share. Before you know it, Cathy thinks Bridget also talked behind her back about her with some other people. Bitterness over this will create more trouble in totally different situations and scenarios.

Cathy, holding on to bitterness, will see it manifest in more places than both thought, even in situations not connected to the original situation. As a matter of fact, it will most likely happen in some other situation simply because of the unadmitted shame that she feels for having resented Bridget, even after the apologies and apparent making up.

Unusual level of interest

When someone suddenly develops a heightened level of

interest in another person's activities, this possibly will be because they feel bitterness. It arises from dislike of the other person. Basing this on the Cathy and Bridget scenario, it is clear that Cathy may perhaps begin to look at Bridget as 'plastic' and she could internally wonder if Bridget was serious about her positive comments about Cathy's new dress.

The true reason as to why there is a question about the other person's actions is simple – bitterness. With time, the person is seen to be up to no good every time they put their hands to a task and, before you know it, the two people will no longer be able to tolerate each other's presence.

Identifying the anger

Whenever someone shows up at a situation, there will be a natural anger and coldness towards that person. It is not usual for strangers in conflicting situations to be openly warm to each other, just like dogs really. It may possibly, at times, not even be intended to be driven at them, but it will naturally appear.

Quite often, resentment becomes coupled with the earlier mentioned embarrassment which arises when someone realises they have no genuine reason to feel what they are feeling. It is simply paranoia!

As a result, there will be increased hostility and coldness to almost everyone present. All this arises from the fact that the anger and bitterness is no longer connected to the original scene, it's now baseless but deeply rooted.

The risk here is that we are putting our own happiness in jeopardy and it will affect all other bonds we have in our lives with other people. It will lead to a situation where someone is generally getting worse and worse by the day.

The idea of bitterness is never really about someone. It could be about a religion, an organisation, a place or even our own selves. For one to overcome this, it is important to determine what the background of the problem really is.

Is it the neighbour you feel bitter about or is it the fact that you were not the first to welcome them to the neighbourhood? Do you feel bitter about school or the very strict lecturer who will not listen to any excuses? In most cases, somehow, there is someone else involved; a person who requires that we forgive them or that we ask for their forgiveness.

Unlike a tango, it does not take to two to forgive. The circumstances of seeking forgiveness may not allow for a direct approach, and sometimes life is stranger than fiction. In these situations you can become the forgiven and the forgiver.

Acting out a ‘forgiveness’ scenario is sometimes the only way you can seek forgiveness, this could be due to you not being able to see the person face to face, or they may have passed away or anyone of a thousand different scenarios.

The main thing is to work from a script, write down your request for forgiveness and then write down the acceptance of it and then put it into action in your mini mind movie.

Use articulated visualisation for this. This method involves using many of your senses. Smell the person’s fragrance as you enter the room, hear the sounds around you and feel the material of the seat you sit on and so on. That way it becomes as real as can be but without you actually being there.

Forgiveness and Love Conquers All

'Without forgiveness life is governed by... an endless cycle of resentment and retaliation'

- Roberto Assagioli

Plan of action

Sit down and ask yourself what exactly caused the bitterness and how you can get over it. Look at the listings below, and be honest with yourself when you look to see what has caused any bitterness.

Letting go of bitterness:

- Accepting that your behaviour is due to some unsettled bitterness and making the decision to actually do something about it.
- Secretly trying to practice anger management, especially to those people you feel bitter about.
- Jotting down the causes of your bitterness and keeping it to yourself.
- Knowing what exactly shows that you are bitter and trying to calm it down.
- Looking at your life as a journey which you should enjoy.
- Writing down the names of the people who have bitterness towards you and trying to forgive some of their wrongs against you.
- Being able to know when you backslide and get back into bitterness.
- Motivating and encouraging yourself to get over previous failures and shortcomings.
- Concentrating where you succeeded but could have done better if you had persisted.
- Hoping to be the best, but not second best.

Getting over bitterness

Step 1

To begin the process of freeing yourself of the bitterness you feel towards someone, you must first know who you have these feelings towards and why you are bitter over them. You can if you so wish provide answers for these questions in your journal:

- Who do you feel bitter over from your early days?
- What did that person do that made you feel bitter towards them?
- What was the magnitude of what they did?
- What has been the effect of your bitterness to these people?
- How has it affected how you live your life and your prospects for the future?
- With all this bitterness, how are you able to live a happy life?

Step 2

After knowing who exactly you feel bitter towards, and how much bitterness has impacted on you, there is a need for you to start a new life and new beginning. In order for this to materialise, you have to be very clear about these questions:

- How is your bitterness stopping you from thinking straight?
- If you healed the feeling of bitterness how would you be able to make a fresh start?
- What will you do to be able to freely

communicate with those you feel bitter about?

- Why are you unable to show your bitterness publicly?
- What are you doing to get over your anger issues?
- Are there new things you have to do so that you can be free of all this anger and bitterness?
- What will you do to avoid the adverse effects of the bitterness?
- How will you benefit from letting go of bitterness?
- What should you do to avoid fresh bitterness from cropping up again?
- How should you conduct yourself after letting go of the bitterness?

Step 3

Since you are now ready to consider a complete overhaul of your life, you need to do a number of things:

- Jot down the names of all the people you have felt bitterness toward even though you may perhaps not tell them.
- Try and decipher why exactly some people treat you the way they do. Are their actions real actions or do you simply conjure them up?
- Render forgiveness to everyone and erase the actions from your mind.

Step 4

When you manage to fully forgive everyone and have erased all those bitter memories from your head, you have to take control of your life and begin to live your life without negativity. This will be the new direction you will take and you should journal it for your records.

Step 5

In the event that your are still stuck in the rather bitter situation that you were in, then you have to redo these steps, carefully, right from Step 1.

CHAPTER 12

EXPEDITE CLOSURE

Forgiveness can be painless

Religion has succeeded in making people feel great respect, compliance and submission to it, but this is not a curative method of doing things. Whatever happens in our lives is not to render punishment to us for anything; it is for us to learn from, but only if we are to make forgiveness part and parcel of our lives. Besides, forgiveness is not about what goes on in other people's lives, it is about what happens in our lives. So we have to look within ourselves for the ability to live a happy and fulfilling life.

'Forgiveness is the sweetest revenge'

- Isaac Friedmann

If we grasp the idea of forgiveness, once and for all, it will benefit you for the rest of your life. Obviously it will require plenty of effort and should not be viewed as some form of self-punishment.

It could happen just once or over a period of time, however we will eventually come to the realisation that we need to alter something in our lives. Naturally, we tend to want to stay close to a thing we are somewhat used to, yet sometimes even that has pain attached to it. Someone who keeps showing up at a place where they are constantly ridiculed may do so simply because they do not want to be 'left out', or another child who keeps tagging along with friends who make jokes about his weight are all examples of people who are stuck in a similar situation. Such scenarios should not be looked upon as punishments but rather as situations that teach us something new each time, as well as helping us to realign our lives.

Numerous reasons are responsible for this trend of events. After looking at how one will benefit after forgiving and forgetting and comparing it with what they will lose if they do not forgive, then it is up to them to sit back and realise which direction they want to take.

Bearing such a concept at the back of your mind will give you a lot of authority over the situation and not allow anyone to walk over you. We have a good number of decisions to make in our lives and it is important for us not to look at these decisions as either positive or negative. In some cases, we possibly will take a certain direction that people will look at as a wrong one, but it is up to us to make good of these situations by learning a thing or two from them.

The faster we incorporate this into our lives, the faster we will get to that fulfilment and eventual happiness that has eluded us for so long.

Doing this is quite effective and will only need you to set aside a few seconds. Personally, it took me a good number of days of using this method for me to realise some improvements within myself. It is worthwhile to know that there is no shortcut to freeing ourselves from all the pain and emotional distress that is caused to us when we have been hurt. However, be rest assured that once we are determined and have our eyes fixed on the ultimate goal, we will realise great progress quite quickly. The success you achieve depends on how much hard work you are willing to put in. Just like in all other aspects of life, the comfort we get from something depends on how much we want to make it that way.

The hidden truth

It is important to let yourself look at the situation impartially and with no distractions. Finding a meditative place where you can do some good thinking would be helpful, however having your mind think impartially is even more helpful. Let everything around you settle down and, for a moment, imagine that you are alone in the world. This is in no way a selfish act because it truly is a moment when you should be dealing with only yourself.

The puzzle to be solved may not have been brought about by you, but you have to think of ways to sort it out all the same. No one else will do it for you even if you put all your hope, prayers and wishes into one basket and cover the problem with them. Doing so will only put a veneer of helplessness over it. If you do not do anything, nothing will happen and if nothing happens, there will be no change. It is a cycle that will keep you stuck in the setback much longer than you think.

Easy strategies

1. Breathe in and out slowly and try to alienate yourself from everything else, bearing in mind the fact that this is YOUR time.
2. When you become composed, start to mention out aloud or simply within the safe confines of your mind, “I Forgive you (mention the person’s name) and I hope you are okay and you do well in life.”

3. To make this a little more impacting, it is good to attach some actions so that you can truly drive the point home. I again say this, there are times when those we are dealing with are not available or not present, therefore it is helpful for us to create or practice scenes of making up with people. Think of yourself hugging them or giving them a good handshake as a sign of making up.
4. Also, if these scenes and people show up often in your life, it helps to let these people appear within your mind. Show them that you bear them no grudge and that you wish them well. By saying this, you are setting yourself on a path of becoming reborn and getting involved in a more outward looking life other than an inward looking one where you are stuck in failing to show everyone that you are stronger, more resilient and even more dependent on yourself. The moment you show people that you can manage to survive on your own emotionally, they will turn to you for solace.

The vital thing here is to detach yourself from all the ill feeling that has taken a fair share of your emotions. It is important to think without influence from resentment or bitterness. For this brief moment, you have all the authority and the ability to sway things in whatever direction you want to. It could be a little difficult because even being honest is almost impossible, however when you do it persistently and consistently you will realise some really great improvements. After sometime, you will tell yourself some of those things and you will smile because you will actually mean them. Sometimes the people you could be in conflict with may well be part and parcel of your life due to reasons even you cannot explain. With time, as you are thankful for the situation that has presented itself, you start to look for some sort of way out of it, and in most cases you will hope and pray that they change their ways.

Enrichment strategy

Whenever you feel any hostility, anger or resentment, you can use the following strategy to enrich yourself. It may well not work the first time or even the first number of times, but that does not mean you should stop using it. Stick to it all the way. There is a need to remember that when you go through a bad situation once, let that be your learning curve so that you do not play the fool next time round. People come into our lives either for a purpose, for a short while or simply to stay.

Being able to look after ourselves is not in any way a sign of individualism or selfishness. There are times when we have to simply push these situations out of our minds and lives. Doing something whose results you are unsure about can be a scary thought but it is worth a try especially if it is an attempt at trying to find a solution to the problem at hand. It will not cost you anything to seek some insight and help from a higher power or source.

You may not secure a resolution with this strategy but it will, at the very least, put you in a position where you can actually see things more clearly. This strategy has helped a good number of people; me included, to generate much needed relaxation and comfort as well as direction and purpose in life.

Personally, it has given me the ability and security to be able to venture into the unknown without fearing getting bruised all over again. Also, it guarantees that I no longer have to do the rather painful thing of approaching the person who hurt me to tell them that I forgive them. It has given me the opportunity to live life with as little worry as possible. A good number of these people may well not reappear anywhere in my life and I have come to terms with this really well.

Being able to forgive people and taking on the healing process is never a simple exercise, however it is paramount for you to know that you have done your best. Assume the authority that you wield. You are worthy of getting better and being peaceful as well as accommodating to new experiences and people. You need not be moved by the acts of other people in your past. The important thing is to grasp the fact that you were meant to learn from this situation and not be tormented by it. This way, you will gain an upper hand on all the feelings of pain and all the people who have caused it alike.

Amidst your bitterness and resentment, there may well be a really bad demon hiding. Any acts of mentioning things or doing things with an aim at causing pain to another person should immediately be denounced so that you can let go of those troubles because they weigh you down.

Responsibility of wrongdoing is something that can cause harm to you, so consequently you have to eliminate it from your life. The only way you can eliminate it is by actually forgiving yourself like you would another person. If some other person is trying to shove guilt down your throat, do not let them have their way. Be answerable for your own actions and acknowledge the fact that what has been done cannot be undone. Try to correct the situation, but always begin by forgiving. Only you can do this. Also, do not be deceived that you are weak because you have forgiven; instead be rest assured that you are now showing great strength - after all, forgiving is onc of the most difficult things to do.

'Forgiveness does not change the past,
but it does enlarge the future'

- Paul Boese

Plan of action

1. Look back to a point in your life when someone needed your forgiveness. Does this situation keep popping up in your mind?
2. Take a note of whatever pops up in your mind and let your body go through all the emotions without any hindrance.
3. Boost your self confidence and talk down your guilt. If for some reason there happens to be no difference, then you need to make a change for the better because you seem to be stuck in the same situation.
4. Closely observe the changes that occur as you go through all the emotional changes that will take hold of you.
5. In the event that you hold on to feelings of being responsible for something that went wrong, you then need to look for a way you can change things.
6. You may not be able to change the past, but you surely are able to make a difference to the future outcome. It is up to you to either take the correct path or continue on the path of guilt.

7. Carry out this practice regularly so that you can let go of the hurt that you are carrying inside of yourself.
8. Handle yourself with great decorum and care and let time heal you through forgiveness.
9. Be sure to pat yourself on the back for achieving this tremendous milestone of forgiveness. Remember, it is not a millstone but a milestone!

CHAPTER 13

CEASE BEING THE VICTIM

True, you may well have been offended and commonly this situation, if left unattended, can be the catalyst to other symptoms like bitterness and paranoia setting in. However, it is useless to keep playing the victim because it will only give room for more hurt and pain. Overly playing the role of the victim can debar you from accepting responsibility for your actions and emotions. Just because you have been through a bad experience does not give you the ticket to keep going back to that situation, over and over again and dramatising it out of proportion.

'The weak can never forgive. Forgiveness is the attribute of the strong'

- Mahatma Gandhi

It is easy to ask yourself the question, "Sincerely, my partner cheated on me and that is not something I can just brush off easily. It is personal." True, your partner could have cheated and it may have hurt you really bad, but you need not take things personally. You need to start using references like, 'Why them' instead of 'Why me'. This will give you an insight into what could have prompted them to act in the way they did. You will come to the realisation that anybody in a similar situation would or could have acted in a similar manner.

By not taking things personally, it is not expected that

you will just sit back and watch things move from bad to worse; neither does it mean that what you are going through is meaningless or a very common occurrence that should be ignored. Look at a situation where many people all over the world have experienced situations similar to or even worse than yours. Once you cease to think of the issue as personal, then you are on your way to getting better through forgiveness of all parties involved.

The idea of always wanting to be the victim in circumstances where you have been offended is a common human trait. Each person wants to be viewed as the aggrieved party. It is within our power to be very warm and inviting, but only when we feel like it. Also, telling people that we have been badly hurt will arouse great sympathy for us and we can find ourselves getting attachment with other people who are aggrieved. So we end up looking at ourselves as badly done to and we see the other people as the wrongdoers who are out to hurt and harm us. However, deep down we are haunted by the worry that no one in particular will offer us the reassurance we need.

Since I am the victim, I will sit back and wait for the other person to make the first move. The sad fact is that this statement is true in many cases and the more we sit back and wait, the more other small things happen that eventually heap up what was initially a very small issue. So if we decide to hold on to the bitterness we are feeling, we are unknowingly blaming the offender, claiming we are the ones who are aggrieved, therefore we need to be sympathised with.

The most important thing we have to know is that by holding on to the sorrow and pain that we are feeling will make us shift the blame on to others. Blaming other people inevitably makes us blame ourselves because if we are pointing the finger at someone, practically, we are pointing it at ourselves as well. Therefore beneath the seemingly victimised person is the true person. When you keep ignoring issues, then you will be stuck in fighting defensive battles.

It is very vital for us to know what exactly is going on within us. The only thing that will make us remain glued to being the victim is our failure to handle the emotions that we go through and the pain that overcomes us. The minute we put aside our self-righteousness and move away from being the aggrieved, then we are on a healing process.

Diving into the sad moments that we have gone through would be a great idea if it would wash away the pain that we are feeling. Sadly this is not how things happen. Sometimes we are very convinced that what we went through needs to be re-lived so we end up going back and forth to the demons of the past and eventually we fail to get over them.

The only way one is bound to get over the emotions is to completely close the chapter that holds them. It may well be a painful thing to do but it certainly is a necessary thing to do. The reason why we fail to detach ourselves from pain and suffering is because we are not willing to go through the pain so that we can eventually get the redemption from the pain.

The idea of forgiveness is a journey that requires patience. If the journey of forgiveness is well travelled, there is a chance that we are bound to change in a very helpful way. The moment we become forgivers, then we are in line to enjoy the benefits of forgiveness. These benefits help us realise how much we are worth and they make us look at a wider perspective of things that will include other people and not just ourselves.

What then is the strategy you are going to embark on so that you can forget the painful past? You have to do some soul searching at the beginning so as to embark on the strategy of forgiveness. Once again, get your journal out and jot down these important questions and answer them candidly:

1. Are you positively sure that you want to offer forgiveness to this person? If you do not, do not be hard on yourself, after all, it is natural. It is much better for you to accept the fact that you are not ready to forgive but make a simple proclamation, 'I forgive'. These feelings inside you need time to sprout. Sometimes we may well feel obliged to forgive someone due to a number of reasons – this too is not correct. Forgiveness is out of your own free will. It is not coerced in any way.

2. Would you like to cease being the victim? In the event that your answer is 'No', then go ahead and ask yourself the question – "Why am I clinging on to all of this bitterness?" Most people are naturally inclined to want to be looked at as the victim in one way or another. We even go as far as wanting everybody else to see us as the aggrieved person so that we can be given some sort of sympathy.

3. One factor that we often forget is that locking ourselves in the situation where we wish for sympathy and want to be looked at as the

aggrieved party normally makes us powerless. If we were to own up to our actions, we would be more resilient and stronger, thus we would persevere in whatever situations come our way.

4. At times we are caught up in the desire to be victims because of our attachments to events and people. For instance, we may perhaps feel obliged to feel some guilt simply because we assess someone as wrongly accusing us of something. In such a situation it is vital to ask yourself the question – "Why do I have to heap all this on myself? Why can't I be happy too?" It is entirely up to you to choose which path to go.

5. If you seriously would like to be released from this situation then you need to bear in mind the fact that you decide your own fate. Therefore you need to first ascertain if you really want to get over whatever is happening. When you do that, you are on the right path.

The idea of forgiveness is not something that will happen within minutes. As already highlighted, for deep-seated situations it will take a great deal of work and lots of commitment and dedication. Obviously, here, we are talking about situations that have caused your life to have some discomfort to it, not the situations that can be remedied by a simple 'sorry'. Saying sorry is a completely different act than seeking forgiveness.

You need to take care of yourself for any kind of healing to take effect. Seek assistance if necessary; the bottom line is you need not feel any loneliness.

'Once a woman has forgiven her man, she must not reheat his sins for breakfast'
- Marlene Dietrich

Plan of action

1. Be ready and free to express how you are feeling and observe that, no matter how bad a scenario may seem, you really gave it your best effort.
2. Be accountable for the decisions you make and if you are the wrongdoer needing forgiveness; be able to point out where you went wrong and how you can correct it.
3. Do not forget that wanting to be looked at as the offended party and thereby seeking sympathy is a decision no one else will make but you.
4. Take full accountability for all the feelings that are aroused inside of you.
5. Take a minute or two to study things carefully and keenly before jumping to conclusions.

CHAPTER 14

FORGIVENESS ASSIGNMENT

Prior to this task, you need to get to a place where you will not be bothered during the course of it. I strongly recommended that you work through this progressively and carry out one task at a time.

'Forgiving is not forgetting. It's letting go of the hurt'
- Anon

Take your time, and if need be get yourself a sheet of paper and write down the questions. Be sure to leave enough room to fit in the answers to the questions. Use a notebook where you can do this work.

- If you really want to be able to get over the issue/s and forgive yourself in all aspects and forms, you have to be able to look back at your journal and pose the question – "What exactly am I feeling responsible for?"

- Take a bold move and go back to your past and look at those situations where you were feeling responsible for certain situations and scenarios. Do not try to block them from resurfacing. If they are communicating with you, give them all the time and space that they require. There could be something in the past that calls for pardoning.

- You may not even have wronged someone but you still harbour some sense of responsibility for what happened. There could also be something that you are embarrassed about from your past; make sure you record it all. This task may possibly have to be redone over and over until you start to feel your guilt burden has been reduced.

The issue of guilt is quite far-reaching and it is very necessary that you handle it with care, making sure that you show great consideration and care for yourself. You will then ask yourself – "Has my guilt affected other people? If so, how? How can I change these things to make them better?" Take a moment and ponder about the whole situation.

Following these steps will ensure that you let go of all the guilt and, as a result, you will have drained a good portion of your energy. Go ahead and pose some questions to yourself:

1. What exactly took place and when did it take place?
2. If the other person and I are at loggerheads, what is the cost to me?
3. What lessons about myself can I pick out from the situation?
4. Has this ever occurred before? How was it that time round? Is there any repetition?
5. Has anyone ever done something like this before?
6. Have I ever caused harm to anyone?
7. In the event that the situation is on-going, what

8. steps can I take to stop it?
9. Who is responsible for the situation?
10. Who caused it?
11. Do I think they are answerable?
12. How did I react when it occurred and what were the effects of the way I reacted?
13. If I could let go of the bitterness, dislike and criticism, what would it feel like?
14. Is there anything I could have done to have averted the situation before it started?

Let your focus drift to the other party. Tell yourself these things about the other person:

1. They want happiness as much as I do.
2. They too would like to steer away from confrontation and tribulations.
3. They too are overwhelmed with bitterness, troubles and unhappiness.
4. They would also like to have their needs and wants attended to.
5. Just like me, they are also simply learning about life.

Do this exercise over again if you have to.

Render forgiveness to yourself. Let the focus shift to YOU. Say these things to yourself:

1. "Making mistakes is a human trait and I am as human as everybody else."
2. "Everyone should be forgiven for the mistakes they make. I too should forgive myself and be

forgiven thereafter."

3. "My previous life will not hold me down. I shall move on."
4. "Life is teaching me lessons and I am an understanding and considerate person."
5. "I decide my own feelings freely and with liberty."
6. "How will I look ahead, look at my choices, set a direction, set fresh targets and venture into new experiences?"

'Forgiveness means that you've decided not to let it keep festering inside even if it only comes up once in a while.'

- Doc Childre and Howard Martin

Plan of action

Bear in mind the fact that it is entirely up to you to keep yourself stuck in bitterness and anger or carry on displaying courtesy and offering and securing forgiveness. Look at the good things about your life and give praise for them. Envision the compassion and feeling that is within you, this will create a good background for the bitterness to evaporate. When you forgive, it is not because we want other people to change. Also when we forgive, the bond may not be restored there and then. It is better to look at forgiveness as a method to make 'ourselves' better. It is born inside of us and does not rely on anyone else's decisions or ideas.

CHAPTER 15

BECOMING COMFORTABLE WITH FORGIVENESS

Partners and forgiveness

In the case of someone hurting another person they are close with, it is logical to say that the two have drifted apart because of the pain and if they are to make up, there should be compromise. Compromise is a settlement of differences by mutual concessions; an agreement reached by adjustment of conflicting or opposing claims, principles, etc by reciprocal modification of demands. So in essence, the word *compromise* means 'a settlement of differences in which each side makes concessions'.

'He who cannot forgive breaks the bridge over which he himself must pass'

- George Herbert

Any such thing like a bond between two people entails that there is extreme care and caution paid to respect for one another, as otherwise, without this, complex and hurtful situations may take place. Reparation to such situations then requires forgiveness to take place, which can, at times, be a slow process.

Being able to forgive yourself is a privilege you enjoy and not for anyone else. It is as simple as asking yourself whether you are ready to use up more of your time and energy pursuing the issue. However, if you are willing to start the healing process, then it is time to say –

"Everything and everyone is forgiven!"

In your mind is the place where the final stages of forgiveness takes place, but first it must start from the heart. It is where you see things looking better up ahead, even after the current pain that is going on. You find yourself having to let go of any ill feelings that you may well be harbouring. When the pains in the heart subside then your mind begins to look at things in a more positive and optimistic way.

Being able to open up to someone about it is an added advantage. This is called having a 'heart to heart', and for good reason. Sometimes forgiving may perhaps not exactly take away the pain. It is not dependant on the other person, it is entirely within you.

It is always up to you to decide which direction to take in terms of forgiveness. It is not really compulsory that you forgive. Getting stuck in the victim mentality, while holding bitterness, therefore refusing to forgive, will most surely make us live a gloomy life. Being vengeful will ensure that more people are hurt.

Start the forgiveness strategy slowly and carefully while keeping concern for the other person's emotions. If you continuously try out forgiveness, eventually you will grasp it and it will help you in many ways.

The general misunderstanding is that once you have forgiven someone, it means that you are okay with what they did. Nothing could be further from the truth. As a matter of fact, forgiveness is rendered to acts that we, at times, do not agree with – wrong acts. Also, forgiving does not necessarily mean that you and the other person are going to make up.

There is another misunderstanding, which is that you only forgive when the other person seeks forgiveness, shows remorse or generally promises to become a better person. If the other person was very bad to you in a way that is a huge part of their day to day life, then they could have you under a spell of pain for a while because they are not going to change in the near future. Being able to forgive comes from within you and is not determined by anything or anyone outside of your close circle.

My view is that when you hesitate to forgive, you still want to act the role of the aggrieved party; after all it is you who decides which direction to take.

Forgiveness is for your own good. Someone you still hold bitterness for possesses you! They practically own you! If in a relationship, after forgiving, it is not compulsory to stay together. This is something you have to decide for yourself.

Obviously the ideal situation would be if they, the wrongdoer, actually approached you to seek forgiveness, but that is only limited to a few people. They may possibly not be ready to take that extra step to seek forgiveness because they may not see the relevance, unless, of course, the affects start to haunt them – something which they have to deal with.

All the pain and sorrow you are feeling will not go if you do not forgive. Being able to get over the pain and render forgiveness will require some time. Sometimes it may take months or even years. Just let it play out naturally. Trying to remember and go over the pain you felt in the past will re-arm the other person while making you defenceless once again. Rather, it would be better if you dwelt more on the 'getting better' process, not the 'getting hurt' process.

It is quite tricky finding out whether you are ready to forgive. Simply ask yourself how fresh the sad memory is in your head. If it still gives you great pain, continue trying to let it go. This may be something that will take you some time to achieve but will leave you feeling better in due course.

'Many people are afraid to forgive because they feel they must remember the wrong or they will not learn from it. The opposite is true. Through forgiveness, the wrong is released from its emotional stranglehold on us so that we can learn from it. Through the power and intelligence of the heart, the release of forgiveness brings expanded intelligence to work with the situation more effectively.'

- David McArthur & Bruce McArthur

The seven steps of forgiveness

Step 1

Begin to exchange ideas when you are no longer as bitter. Get a place that will suit you both and not make you tense. Put away or turn off all distractions like phones, the TV and anything else that may perhaps distract you.

i) The first time, although you may possibly want to let out everything that is on your mind, however it is wise to go slow, sorting out one issue at a time.
ii) Let your partner talk to you at their own pace and discretion.
iii) Let the time you spend together occur automatically.
iv) Do not worry about how long it will take. You need all the time.
v) Look at each other in the eye and be sure to show them that you are ready to bring things out in the open so that you can settle issues.

Forgiveness and Love Conquers All

'Know all and you will pardon all'

- Thomas A'Kempis

Step 2

Listen a lot more than you speak. Let them express themselves without you telling them what to do. This could in fact be one of the reasons for your disagreements – because you are always 'offering advice'.

When we forgive, we are freed from the demons of our past and we head to a brighter future. It is not that we forget what happened; it is just trying to look at the future with optimism and the promise of a better and brand new day.

What is behind will not help us move forward. If you want to live in peace and harmony with your partner, it is important that you let go of the past.

Make a fresh start! There is no way you can start afresh unless you let go of the bitterness and pain inside of you. This can slow down your journey to happiness because they create paranoia and will leave you worried about reoccurrence of such situations. Therefore it is important to properly grasp the issue of forgiveness.

Forgiving means 'giving up' or 'letting go'. It could also refer to getting oneself back to your former good self. You let go of bitterness and desire for vengeance, start to believe in life once again and whoever does not do so is bound to get hurt or affected in a negative way.

'Sincere forgiveness isn't coloured with expectations that the other person apologize or change. Don't worry whether or not they finally understand you. Love them and release them. Life feeds back truth to people in its own way and time'— just like it does for you and me.'

-Sara Paddison

i) Take some time and just listen attentively. If you do not understand something, ask the other person to explain. Offer support but do it with regard for the other person
ii) If your partner's judgment is clouded by sentiment, carefully remind them of your concerted agreement to be as objective as possible with the intention to forgive
iii) As you listen, be keen about your own emotions. Stay clear of anything that may well make you clash in any way.
iv) Try and hear out your partner as they narrate their side of the story.
v) Do not let your sentiment cloud your judgement. Dedicate everything to your partner, because at a certain time you will require that they too dedicate everything to you.

'Humanity is never so beautiful as when praying for forgiveness, or else forgiving another'

- Jean Paul

Step 3

As a keen listener, your role is over when they finish telling their side of the issues. It now becomes your turn to let your feelings be known. It is your opportunity to put your point across.

If you are at loggerheads with other people, there is no way you can have any harmony within yourself. You need to dig deep and let the bitterness fade, it will not take a lot of energy but it will need you to summon up a lot of courage. Your forgiveness or failure to forgive simply takes you nearer or further away from your ultimate goal. There are no two ways to deal with it, there is only one.

If you want harmony and tranquillity, you are going to have to forgive. The same zeal and guts with which you were persistent not to forgive is the same zeal and enthusiasm with which you should be able to open up a new relationship with your partner, loved one or friend, one that is founded on commitment and dedication.

The issue of forgiveness is probably the one and only single thing that will offer you tranquillity. Each person has encountered some pain and sadness. Some people have even gone ahead to conclude that they can *not* forgive. They feel hurt so much that they become hostile and bitter, which makes forgiveness all the more difficult.

Having a life that is not free of bitterness and resentment is very taxing. It can make you get darker and darker on the inside because all the bad feelings and emotions are locked up inside your heart. In such a situation, forgiveness is really a necessity. Obviously it will not be easy, but that should not deter you from your ultimate goal.

Forgiving is not a scheduled item we must achieve, it is a process that we must let run within us. If we let our spirit take control and direct our thoughts and emotions towards forgiveness, we will, in most cases, realise that forgiveness is a beautiful thing to do because we shall be feeling rejuvenated and renewed with special feelings of freshness and warmth. We then become free and can process all these great feelings towards making those around us smile too.

Being able to forget the past and move forward is something that will, in most cases, give the forgiver a great boost.

Offer yourself forgiveness as a gift. The word ‘give’ is

the basic keyword in the word *forgiveness*, therefore it relays a meaning therein. When you forgive, you are freed from some of the feelings of disapproval and it can contribute to lessening your negative thoughts. When you forgive, it does not mean that you have submitted, it simply means that you have made a choice to stop bearing any grudge. Therefore you cease to be a hateful figure and it purifies you of any ill will, hurt and pain. No one else is accountable for the decisions you make.

'I can forgive, but I cannot forget, is only another way of saying, I will not forgive. Forgiveness ought to be like a cancelled note - torn in two, and burned up, so that it never can be shown against one.'

- Henry Ward Beecher

i) Proper, honest and genuine communication is a key factor. Communicate to your partner that you are well versed and in sync with the exact particulars of the situation.
ii) Let your sentiments come out. Be as expressive as possible and do not hide away feelings from your partner. Also, when they come out, do not continue to pursue or hang on to them.
iii) Be slow and sure about your own communication. The other person will appreciate the fact that you need time to be able to properly express yourself as clearly as possible.
iv) Let the other person know that your part is done when you are sure they have grasped what you have to say.

'Forgiveness means letting go of the past'

- Gerald Jampolsky

Step 4
It is possible for you to forgive someone but then fail to forget the misdemeanour that led up to or caused the situation. Today you may well offer forgiveness and then some days later, the pain stings you again. At such times when the pain creeps in, remind yourself that you offered the person full forgiveness. If you have to, forgive them all over again, and then carry on going forward. With time, the pain you feel will slowly lessen and before you know it, the pain will become a distant memory.

Just like any other normal human being, you are prone to hurting and being hurt. The important thing to note is that amidst all this you need to emerge with some kind of lesson learned from the situation. If you do this, then you are on the way to forgive.

Your life's joy and happiness depends on forgiveness. It requires for you to be brave and courageous to be able to render forgiveness and when you do it, you will have created reconciliation as well as transformed sadness and gloom in to happiness and joy.

Forgiveness is no different from love, but from a different perspective. Forgiving is offering love to your enemy. Forgiving out of obligation is as selfish as can be.

'Not the power to remember, but its very opposite, the power to forget, is a necessary condition for our existence.'

- Sholem Asch

i) If you are the wrongdoer, do not hesitate to seek forgiveness.
ii) In case the injured party is not yet willing or ready to forgive, do not rush them. Just be

optimistic and give them all the time they need. At times, healing from certain situations can take a bit of time.

iii) Phrase this in your own words and say them to the injured party, "I ask that you please forgive me for the wrong that I have done you. My wish is that you can find it in your heart to say I am forgiven for causing you pain."

iv) When you firmly and boldly ask for forgiveness, you will actually heal whoever is involved; the wrongdoer and the one feeling the pain.

'Forgiveness is the key to action and freedom'

- Hannah Arendt

Step 5
Forgiving your companion

When you forgive, you immerse yourself in healing waters. Maintaining a situation that is not repaired means your life can be a misery, not because of what happened to you moments or months back; but because of what is happening to you right now.

It has been proven over time that when someone feels so immensely hurt, they will most likely feel much better if they offered the other person forgiveness both outside and within.

When you forgive, you cease to be within the endless bitterness, ill feeling, displeasure and suffering that spreads to whoever is near you. When you forgive, you come to terms with whatever is behind you. That is when you can go forward with a clear conscience and start living a carefree and worry free life.

Forgiveness and Love Conquers All

The importance of forgiveness

Forgiveness gives you the opportunity to make a fresh start. Noting down all the particulars of a particular situation that left you feeling some pain is an important aspect of coming to terms with what happened and to creating a new beginning to moving forwards. The way you note things down will determine how you go about the whole process of forgiveness.

If you note down the advantages you saw from a bad situation, instead of the feelings you felt or just noting down something entirely not connected at all, it will be a move in the right direction in terms of forgiving and carrying your life forward. Journaling, perhaps, is going to be your pathway to forgiveness more than you thought.

'Forgiveness is a funny thing. It warms the heart and cools the sting'

-William A Ward

i) When you have been wronged, forgive at such a time as when you are ready.
ii) The heart is where the journey of forgiveness begins, "I sincerely forgive you and I know you did not intend to cause me any hurt or pain." (Exchange for your own words. Be honest about it.)
iii) If you do not feel ready to forgive yet, "Please give me a little more time to get a hold of my feelings. I am thankful for your apology but I just need some time to able to accept it fully and wholly." (Again, use your own words.)
iv) When the time comes and you are ready, forgive your partner immediately.

'Forgiveness is the giving, and so the receiving of life'
- George MacDonald

Step 6
When you have forgiven, carry on and do not look back. Talk about how you can keep away from hurting each other again. Talk about all the things that you think need readjustment so that the relationship can be peaceful.

You may not condone what they did to you, but take some time to walk in their shoes. When you empathise, mostly for men, there is great forgiveness that can be rendered; moreover easily. Once you cease to look at them as 'the enemy' then you are bound to fully grasp issues concerning them.

Hanging on to bitterness and ill will drains you so much for no good reason. Handling a situation like that may well turn out to be a hurtful one and could graduate in to more dangerous situations.

Bear in mind the fact that the other person also has good qualities which you need to concentrate on. Try to give them the benefit of the doubt and look at their intentions so as not to create any hurt or harm, except if you have real tangible evidence that their intentions were really nefarious. If you give them the benefit of the doubt, you are bound to find it easier to offer them forgiveness.

'You will know that forgiveness has begun when you recall those who hurt you and feel the power to wish them well.'

- Lewis B Smedes

i) Being in harmony and keeping on the same page are quite vital if you are to achieve anything.

ii) Be ready to practice the emotion you feel for each other. Hugging and kissing or holding hands is a great follow up to forgiving, but it should not keep you from showing more love a little later. Be unpredictable, be charming and be kind to one another. Do not hold anything back.

iii) What you see as 'good' or 'nice' may possibly not be the same to other people. Therefore if there are some bad traits about you, be considerate with your partner and do away with them.

iv) Get into the habit of being thankful. Be thankful for what you share with your partner and remind yourselves to thank one another for being a part of each other's lives.

v) Maintain an interest in your own situation and make this clear.

'Forgiveness is the economy of the heart... forgiveness saves the expense of anger, the cost of hatred, the waste of spirits.'

- Hannah More

Step 7

Forgiving is not the last piece of the puzzle. You need to give time for the bond to be rebuilt. We all *err* and we all have off days. We all mention things that may well hurt those we love but actually do not really mean. We all have to forgive and deserve to be forgiven.

There is no bond between two people that can exist and survive without forgiveness. It may perhaps be difficult, but forgiveness is vital in a marriage or partnership between the sexes. Harbouring grudges will only lead to a breakdown of the relationship.

'What we forgive too freely doesn't stay forgiven'
- Mignon McLaughlin

i) Trust is a very easily broken link and can only be made strong by respect for one another and loyalty. After forgiveness, you get better and the trust gets re-established.
ii) The moment you start to remember the situation or event that hurt you, let your mind head off to a calm and relaxing place or find an activity to occupy your mind.
iii) Do not reawaken ghosts of the past by reminding your partner about the errors they made as a way to get back at them for something.
iv) Try not to punish your partner in any way, it will make things worse.
v) Sometimes the true reason for a certain hurtful situation may never be uncovered. Accept this fact.
vi) Always bear in mind the fact that when you forgive, you may not be exactly okay with what your partner did.
vii) Do not rush to forgive your partner. Take as much time as you need.
viii) If you never seem to be ready to forgive or realise that you are always thinking about how hurtful certain situations were, talk to a professional counsellor.
ix) Forgiveness should be founded on your desire to make things better and to grow within yourselves.
x) Be conscious about your relationship and it will help your continued growth and realisation that you are both wonderful creatures who love and

trust one another.

xi) Forgiveness is greatly founded on patience.

xii) Sympathy is an important aspect of forgiveness. Look at the compassion, excellence and appeal that surround you. It is all around you, sometimes you have to readjust yourself to realise it. To be good to others, you first need to be good to yourself.

A good relationship is rather difficult if there is no forgiveness. If you cling on to past happenings, there is a great chance that you will not manage to sustain a fulfilling relationship at all. If you want to live a happy and fulfilled life, you have to be in harmony with your siblings, ex lovers, colleagues, children and whoever else may well have wronged you.

You can only make a current relationship work right if you make sure your previous events and situations do not hurt you over and over again.

When you forgive someone, you have made the decision to let go of any wrong they did against you. You have to give them the benefit of the doubt, there is no other alternative.

You may well say in disbelief, “How do I give them the benefit of the doubt when they did something as bad as that to me? No way!” You have to simply let bygones be bygones.

Failure or refusal to forgive will leave you fighting. Once you forgive, calmness and harmony will be restored.

When you forgive, you regain your composure, self-respect, confidence and enthusiasm. In an unforgiving world, chaos rules.

'Don't tell friends their social faults; they will cure the fault and never forgive you'

\- Logan Pearsall Smith

Plan of action

The moment any sentiments of pain or bitterness show up, try various strategies like relaxation, stress management, meditation, yoga, art, dance, massage and even music. Let your energy be directed towards doing things that you actually love to do other than directing it to the hurt you feel.

CLOSING REMARKS

When you have been hurt, it is rather easy to heap blame on others. This whole process is aimed to stop you from looking at others and to start looking at yourself as the beginning of the healing process after getting hurt.

'Without deep humility, true forgiveness is impossible ... and will never happen'

- Martha Kilpatrick

Forgiveness is the solution to ill will, resentment, pain, bitterness, sadness and hostility. For true healing to occur, you must be ready to be true and honest. Simply mentioning it with lip service will not make things better, it will actually make them worse by heaping more guilt on to you.

Real and genuine forgiveness comes from deep inside of the heart. It does not matter what you say, but how you deliver what you say that creates recovery after pain.

A good number of people feel a sense of completion and closure when forgiveness is done up-close, face to face, however this may perhaps not be the case for everyone. Someone may well not need to appear in front of you for you to render forgiveness. You can just do it inside your heart. The reaction and response of the other person should not affect your ability to forgive. It is entirely your decision to make.

When you forgive someone, do not think that you should feel better there and then. It may well take time but it will come. All the sorrow and pain you feel inside of you will leave you eventually. When you stop holding on to it, it will stop holding on to you.

You are the custodian of your own happiness. What other people say, do or think does not create a basis for your happiness. It is you who decides your own happiness, just like forgiveness.

When you make up your mind to forgive, your happiness will almost automatically follow. When you forgive, your life carries on, only getting better. This is your chance to concentrate on important things in your life. It is true, you may possibly not easily forget what happened previously but you can make your life ahead much better. Forgiveness does not change the past, that's for sure, but it does change the future.

Other Titles by Mirage Publishing

Paperback Non-fiction Books

A Prescription from The Love Doctor: How to find Love in 7 Easy Steps - Dr Joanne 'The Love Doctor' Coyle
Burnt: One Man's Inspiring Story of Survival - Ian Colquhoun
Cosmic Ordering Guide - Stephen Richards
Cosmic Ordering: Sex Energy - Stephen Richards
Cosmic Ordering: You can be Successful - Stephen Richards
Die Laughing: War Humour from WW1 to Present Day - George Korankye
Hidden Secrets: Attract Everything You Want! – Carl Nagel
Internet Dating King's Diaries: Life, Dating and Love – Clive Worth
Life without Lottie: How I survived my Daughter's Gap Year - Fiona Fridd
Mrs Darley's Moon Mysteries: A Celebration of Moon Lore and Magic – Carole Carlton
Mrs Darley's Pagan Elements: A Celebration of Air, Fire, Water, Earth and Divine Spirit – Carole Carlton
Mrs Darley's Pagan Whispers: A Celebration of Pagan Festivals, Sacred Days, Spirituality and Traditions of the Year – Carole Carlton
Rebel Diet: They Don't Want You to Have It! – Emma James
The Real Office: An Uncharacteristic Gesture of Magnanimity by Management Supremo Hilary Wilson-Savage - Hilary Wilson-Savage

The Tumbler: Kassa (Košice) – Auschwitz – Sweden - Israel - Azriel Feuerstein (Holocaust survivor)

Paperback Inspiration Mini-series
Boost Your Self-esteem – Stephen Richards
Overcoming Procrastination – Stephen Richards
Overcoming Self-limiting Beliefs – Stephen Richards
Unbeatable Self-confidence – Stephen Richards

Paperback fiction Books
I Can See Clearly Now The Rain Is Gone - George Korankye. This incorporates a factual event of the Dunblane massacre into a highly sensitive work of faction.

E-Books
7 Day Focusing Plan - Stephen Richards
Boost Your Self Esteem – Stephen Richards
Forgiveness and Love Conquers All: Releasing You from the Past - Stephen Richards
Overcome Procrastination – Stephen Richards
Overcoming Self Limiting Beliefs – Stephen Richards
Think Your Way to Success - Stephen Richards

Cosmic Ordering Series ***CD& MP3***
Cosmic Ordering Connection - CD& MP3 Stephen Richards
Cosmic Ordering: Chakra Clearing - CD& MP3 Stephen Richards
Cosmic Ordering Meditation (The Ultimate series) – CD& MP3 Stephen Richards
Cosmic Ordering: Rapid Chakra Clearing – CD& MP3 Stephen Richards

The Ultimate Cosmic Ordering Meditation CD& MP3 Stephen Richards

Releasing You From series *CD& MP3*

Releasing You From Fear CD& MP3 Stephen Richards

Releasing You From Insomnia CD& MP3 Stephen Richards

Releasing You From Social Anxiety CD& MP3 Stephen Richards

Releasing You From The Past CD& MP3 Stephen Richards

The Ultimate series *CD& MP3*

The Ultimate 10 Minute Chakra Clearing CD& MP3 Stephen Richards

The Ultimate Change Your Life Guided Meditation CD& MP3 Stephen Richards

The Ultimate Confidence & Ego Boost CD& MP3 Stephen Richards

The Ultimate Focus Builder CD& MP3 Stephen Richards

The Ultimate Inner Self Link Up CD& MP3 Stephen Richards

The Ultimate Power of Positive Thinking CD& MP3 Stephen Richards

The Ultimate Self Hypnosis CD& MP3 Stephen Richards

The Ultimate Stop Smoking CD& MP3 Stephen Richards

The Ultimate Success in Love CD& MP3 Stephen Richards

Stephen Richards

The Ultimate Wealth Creation CD& MP3 Stephen Richards
The Ultimate Weight Loss CD& MP3 Stephen Richards

See these titles at:
www.miragepublishing.com
&
www.cosmicordering.net